PORTRAIT
OF US
BURNING

PORTRAIT OF US BURNING

poems

SEBASTIÁN H. PÁRAMO

Curbstone Books / Northwestern University Press
Evanston, Illinois

Curbstone Books
Northwestern University Press
www.nupress.northwestern.edu

Printed in the United States of America

10 9 8 7 6 5 4 3 2 1

Library of Congress Cataloging-in-Publication Data

Names: Páramo, Sebastián H, author.
Title: Portrait of us burning : poems / Sebastián H. Páramo.
Description: Evanston, Illinois : Curbstone Books/Northwestern University Press,
    2024.
Identifiers: LCCN 2023025326 | ISBN 9780810146488 (paperback) |
    ISBN 9780810146495 (ebook)
Subjects: LCSH: Mexican Americans—Poetry. | Mexican American families—
    Poetry. | LCGFT: Poetry.
Classification: LCC PS3616.A728 P67 2024 | DDC 811.6—dc23/eng/20230530
LC record available at https://lccn.loc.gov/2023025326

For my family

CONTENTS

II. Burning

PORTRAIT
OF US
BURNING

WHERE YOUR FATHER WAS

for my Uncle Lalo

We lent each other tools. We learned the American tongue.
We wing-manned & learned "Dancing on the Ceiling."

We showed off our phrase, our bailas con el amor.
We gave the shove, said here's a job patching roofs.

We scaffolded frames. We built homes.
We woke at dawn, kissed our wives, our newborns—

We sent money back home. We remembered where our father worked.
Once,

there was a power plant—he raised us
on one knee. He said there's a whole sky waiting.

Take its clouds, its rain, & drink it. We take that cloud.
We save it for thirsty hearts. We gave it to you.

I

PORTRAIT OF US

There is no one who
will feed the yearning.
Face it. You will have
to do, do it yourself . . .

—Gloria E. Anzaldúa, "Letting Go"

PORTRAIT OF MY FATHER AS A FAILED ROMANTIC

My father ran away as a young man / He leapt across the Rio
He slept inside the trunk of a Camino

He didn't know English but I found books in his closet
His American songbook & his acoustic guitar   sat lonely

like his eyes // staring at his father's workbench
Then his first son was born
                Then   I—his second son was born
My mother calls him   [*teenager, vagrant, perro—ojos sin vergüenza*]

I'm older than when he became a father,
        I wonder what he misses
Because I'm not him // I recognize his inheritance is my closet.
                I sold the guitar . . . he gifted me

& yet   I call him when I want something
He wants to provide nothing
but the best   —he took us on trips to AstroWorld
[He always wanted a playground]

He never wondered—what if he wasn't [here]
But I do   I *do* wonder   He says he's seen   his life
flash before his eyes

His hair, jeans, and blazer slicked back   his heavy cologne
Larger than his childhood   wider than his father's fields of wheat //

Where was *his* father's song?   When my father looks away
        He's a younger man turned everlasting

DIEGO RIVERA, *THE FLOWER CARRIER*, 1935

He kneels under the burden of flowers.
Looking down, he cannot feel their beauty.
The purple heft weighs him down.
His yellow sling used to latch the cradle
of picked ones feels flimsy
as if it could slip off   like a scarf, a dress.

The woman, do you see how she holds steady,
with strong arms, their bounty. While he, he's bent
on all fours pushing the earth, she is watching him
struggle, she looks down upon him.

Under the brim of his hat, under the dark
shade, under the voice of rustled overgrown leaves,
I can only imagine the cost of not coming up.
Where does the basket go after he stands
again with the flowers, unloading their lightness?

Thorn-trimmed by hand. He takes them to florists,
the market, the woman who held him steady.
Each one is pressed then gently inside the folds
of books read by candlelight.

Once, in my childhood home,
a copy of Rivera's painting hung in the kitchen
& while I read under the covers about his life,
I wondered about the man: how he carried
loads each night, too exhausted to finish anything
but carrying flowers. Did he dream about petals he found
stuck in his lapel, pressed inside his shoes, the way they stained
his clothes? How the soft earth wore his linen knees
when he kneeled again & again to lift a new basketful?

Did my father and mother wonder how the man must wash
these white clothes each day, carefully by hand? How he scrubbed
& scrubbed the dirt out, to feel opulent each morning, to honor his labor.

SELF-PORTRAIT AS MY FATHER, THE ROOFER

I work hard heat into a home.
                    Then when everything is done & dark,

I lie flat & can't help thinking of those
                    who named stars. Because there once was a
                    city I fled.

It lived in my brow while I crossed the Rio
                    & stared at the Big Dipper. The past talked
                    to me,

& stars read like a possible world, a legend on a map
                    waiting to be found—always there, guiding.

Now, this unbearable sky tars my roof.
                    The cooler of beers, the hours waged, the meals

brought to a table with calloused hands—
                    led to my first love: a blue-green

Chevrolet truck. I will gift it to my son for nothing.
                    He earned it when he gave me a North Star.

I will lead him by his hand to the flatbed
                    & we'll look toward a swath of stars. We'll call
                    it ours.

We'll draw Orion, Ursa Major
                    We'll lay our floor plans. We'll build a home

over & over again until it feels solid enough
                    to dust off our boots & walk inside.

Your mother brought tiny shampoo bottles home.
      She probably brought the spare sheets too.
You lived in a one-bedroom apartment, the three of you.
      (Tu Mamá, Tu Papá, y tu.)

Whenever Dad was home, you ate junk food & watched *Tales from
      the Crypt.*
You built forts. Your mother didn't like the idea of you alone.

She hovered saint-like over the bed. Never awake to hear the door open,
I suppose she stepped into your room and her heart overflowed with
      prayer.

Never did I imagine she might have a rude guest or change the sheets of
      a couple
who just fucked. She was close to elegance. Polishing gold.

You said you dreamed she spent evenings in the presidential suite.
The work wasn't for anyone else but her family because she dreamed

her firstborn would inherit the house. & she used to love sitting by
      the pool,
getting her feet wet until you & your father came along.

I was small when mother got the belt & whooped the bad out.
She'd rocked my boyhead, saying *I'm sorry, I'm sorry*,
back & forth until she drove her Ford Taurus to serve lunch
at the high school. Back & forth, she dropped us off & lifted us.
Until her car was T-boned on the way to school one morning.
We were late that day. She remained calm amidst the traffic.
The man said, *I'm sorry, I'm sorry.* He called someone
to fix our situation & she didn't say anything but *thank you.*
When I was small, I misheard the gym teacher call me *stupid.*
What he said: *stop it* because I was acting up—
my mother's English was upset, speaking with the principal,
asking *how, how, how?* The gym teacher's face asked *why, why, why*
did I hear that? I asked why they insisted
I speak to the ear, nose & throat specialist. What I heard
back then—how could my senses be so mistaken?
I once mistook my mother for a hotel maid,
I thought she brought shampoo bottles home after cleaning
presidential suites. My memory was wrong.
It was other people's rich homes.
At one woman's home, she sometimes stayed & watched their small boy
—& I couldn't believe it wasn't me. I'm sorry, Mother.
I didn't know how much you dreamed
of cutting strangers' hair, turning clients in a chair around,
so they saw your beauty salon certificate behind you.
[She's done it before with me.] Their hair, a work of art by her fingers.
Why did her dream burn down one day,
before I could ask *what was your dream, Mamá, before you cleaned houses?*
My mother learned to drive the stick shift on a white Firebird,
her mistakes, an unlearning, revving like a Firebird.
Wherever we drove, she recounted the Greyhound
from Celaya, city of cajeta. How bittersweet
her last trip—we flew there long ago,
visited her parents before they died.

Did they know what she burned for?
How she left the washing machine factory & danced in Texas.
Their remains were cremated.
What's left is their ashes
& what my mother tells me.
Some mistakes you can't control.
She met my father one night
& learned who he was—a former smoker.
A man of furious passion for family.
Their ghosts can't help
telling you about flames. They flicker like glitches,
                        near misses with God
                        & you remember there's brimstone
                        & fallen angels have room for forgiveness.

Oh, Phoenix, let my mother be a bird.

SELF-PORTRAIT OF THE FIRSTBORN'S QUESTIONS

What did Mother want back then?

    A faithful man?
    A provider?

Brother,   did you ever wonder as I did?
If he loved your mother & mine?

Brother,   did you know that I ask so many questions:
If I am the expression of infidelity, the second want?

If I wasn't meant to arrive, did our father ask

if he could
go back & unfather me?

FOOTAGE OF US PLAYING

Dad says *this is your brother.*
      Go play. I play with his toys.

[*Not mine. Not Ours.*]
      I'm told we're blood.

My first hinge:
      blood

blooms & glows
      in the doorway:

My brother knocked my head there.
      An orange static haze. Hospital

stitches.
      The snow of G's TV set

tracks me—a VCR plays us.
      (   )

This is Father watching us play.
      Hit replay.

I didn't know G's mother would
      blame me

& point a pistol
      at our window.

Dad takes me from him.
      My first brother.

How do you want us, Father?
　　　　How do we become

two happy households?
　　　　We're only two brothers.

[Balled-up fists]
　　　　Hurting for the same bed.

WATCHING *THE LION KING* WITH MY FATHER

(dir. Rob Minkoff & Roger Allers)

It was the first movie I remember watching in a theater.
The one with two screens on Walnut Road. I sat back there.
I ate popcorn. An opening shot of an animated savannah.
The lions hold the future king above the fertile kingdom.

Everything the light touches signifies an ownership.
This will be yours one day. I eat kernels of this image.
These animated stills. Isn't that nice for a young boy to eat up?
          One day you'll inherit the kingdom of your parents.

          Only in the dark corner of kingdoms, there are hyenas.
Those who won't care about you. My father said, survival of the fittest.
They will take advantage of you, if you don't—
What he taught me was that family can betray you. They ask for money.

They ask for pieces of paradise. Wrapped in care packages.
Mailed to Mexico. All the old things. Even if it's his last dollar,
my father becomes bitter about love. We leave the theater
thinking about kingdoms. We point at stories in the night skies.

The stars tell me what I want to hear. The ancestral plain reads
my heart. I can't hide what the earth feels in my footsteps.
I always wondered where I'd find someone who recognizes me.
          Lately, I don't recognize the child inside—because I'm finally
          learning who I am.

My kingdom is me. This acre of skin I wear & I must love because
the light touches me every day. Someone told me it's hard to desire
          kingdoms.
It's hard when someone else wants what you want. Even when you're
          blood.
My father warned me. My mother warned me. I don't remember when

I finally paid attention. I finally learned I can't help loving kingdoms.
Even when my father is gone, it's unspoken. Remember blood.
The blood. Its unconditional nature. DNA won't leave. It won't leave
the machine. It haunts me. I pass it down a river: a basket that's a part
    of my life,

no worries. I learned this on my own.
    I hit replay watching a son lose his father.
I hit replay. It happens again. Brothers will betray you.
    I look over my shoulder.
Mufasa. I hit replay. I see myself in a pool.
    It took me too long to understand
letting go. I embrace what happens & I don't hit pause.
    When Mufasa succeeded,

he ruled over the kingdom. Darkened it. Until it was so gray & ugly
that we needed the light again. Except, I have a brother. I want him to
    forgive me.
I want to forgive him. I want to grow old & yellow & forgive him.

HIBISCUS

If we roughhouse as brothers,
we bleed & eat dirt. Younger days,
we took fistfuls of teeth & held on tight.

Wet mouth nuzzling my neck.
Animal sibling. Mud & breath of dog days.
We knew each other. We traded cards & punches.

Collected frogs at dusk in Duck Creek Park.
We step into it again. More wolf than cub now.
Ash & lime on Tecate cans. Al pastor

on tortilla flats, burning. Charred. The touch
of white frosting on birthdays. Purpled creeks at night
after everyone ate. Swollen belly. I can't move.

I'm full & afraid of a time we won't jab & be cruel
with love. I was once a wolf baring his teeth.
I licked the salt off my lips & trembled to know

the ache of soft ruby petals in my mouth.
Hibiscus boiled. We must drink now like brothers.
Let us make a pact. Let us reign over the woods again.

Let us eat the flesh of game. We must devour spirits so dark
they glow like worms & burn & steep in a kettle
until every winter becomes dire with its whistle.

DEAR FATHER

What was the secret—
my brother's home: a trailer park?

      What if memory
was white noise, a cable box, searching for the right channel.

In 1992, what do I know of family?
      If I could find the right one,
or rewind the tape.

      Except,
      I regret watching you arrested because
                    your ex-wife—her gun.

                 Her portrait of family,
         shattered.
There is no father,   like you,   living at home.

You shouldn't have brought me here.

[Insert portrait of *Freedom from Want* by Norman Rockwell here.]

In the apartment complex parking lot,
      your ex has come to point her gun at your *other* family.
      Her freedom from your want.

That scene was *us* weighing desire.
      Your family, under the warm lighting,

      the bunk bed we all slept in.
      You, me, Mom, hungry bellies—hungering.

We didn't know what would come.
The night you were arrested for our domestic
            disturbance—I put my childhood on pause.

I fast forward & rewind. Eject.
            Father versus Mother-I-Don't-Know.

            [The pistol in her drawer.]

            [Mother of your other firstborn.]

The police arrive after she's done pointing
her pistol at me in a window, I laugh

in the hallway at age five because I didn't know who I was.
I wanted to have something funny like *Ernest Goes to Jail*:

Isn't it funny? My Daddy is in jail.

& my Daddy comes home & we forget it happened.
We tape over the memory like it was a bad joke.

SELF-PORTRAIT AS HALF-SIBLING

Not my father's son. They tell me, *I am doubt.*
I am full of it. *I am not this blood.* More like
my mother, I have her face. Her hair.

I am my mother's son. To know my brother
means knowing *his* mother's face & our
father's too. It means, I was young enough

to be told, I'm not man enough to wear *family*
alone—he wants us to each own a bit of himself.

I feel like I do not belong to him alone.

But we cannot be family. There was an accident:
G snaps open my head once,

playing rough because there must be
one better brother. Doctors stitch my skin
as if there were a thread between us.

We bleed in this split-in-two household.
We do not share toys. We do not share a mother,
no, we are suspicious bunkmates, one-upping

our affection for home until the last straw:
the missed phone call that says I am still here.

We are family. You are here &
you are the blood tied at the ankle, the buried foot.

DIPTYCH: DAYS OF THE LATCHKEY

I

His mother paints over his fatherly image.

Her words: cobarde, cobarde / get out of the house.
Mira, mira, he'd say. I love you. Like a snake, she'd say.

Tell me who you are.
Dígame, dígame. His father asks in the car.

His mother asks the other woman on the phone.
    Vibora, vibora / Serpiente. The other woman is a coward

        under heat. June—it's Father's Day.
        It's your father's birthday. Ask him what he wants.

    Be nice to your brother. / He's living with us this summer.
    Be nice to my mother. / She lives with us.

    Give him what he doesn't deserve.
    Your mother never says. Nobody ever says.

Your brother never stays long.

II

    Listen, your brother is playing nice.
    Listen, your father & brother are watching an R-rated movie.

You're too young.
You have to share.
    You lie, cheat, and steal from each other.
    You think brothers are awful.

You say you're adopted.
You say you're bastards.

Like brothers, we watch *Maury* together.
Like brothers, we consider paternity tests.

    Are you my brother?

Watch how the cameras follow the MOTHERS.
That's not your father.

        That never happened.
        Your mother leaves you, the boys at home.

Let them sit quiet, cross-legged, not fighting,
Let them ask if their father wanted this all along.

He's not here.
He's working so he won't be afraid.
He's working so hard to fail upward
& now I'm being charmed by snakes in my adult life;

        I'm leaving lovers behind.
My brother won't have children.

        We locked our childhood in a safe.
I'm asking you to keep that memory, a goosebump on your back.

PORTRAIT OF RIVALRY

I'm ashamed to be in this family.
        Because he lied to my mother,

because she taught me
        to hate *him*. [Half-brother] I scroll back

to family road trips:
        Galveston, Orlando,

the rental car we drove counting license plates
signs to the theme parks.

Along the highway,
I dream of a family.

My brother too.
I rest my head on the window

reading the signs—I count
        billboards of family vacations.

Sometimes, I picture
        a different family's backseat

& bickering is strange,
we're not begging for Father's attention.

When I drive now,
        I look at the rear-view.

I try.
        I try not to forget the rivalry.

Wasn't it a strange house? // The swimming pool was above ground. // Streamers & party horns. // Party whistles for the little ladies popping balloons. // Un pastel de tres leches. // Would you like fruit with your sugar? // Insulin medication. // What do clowns say? You act like one. // How about a pitcher of Kool-Aid? // Isn't it strange, the stereo plays, mumbled in the background? // We sound like underwater people. Like we're wet. // Why are we family with these people? Why are they walking away now? They don't want you here, walking in their shadows, smoking their cigarettes. It's annoying to say she's with him. Your dad is talking about your ex-girlfriend. For some reason, he says she cheated on you. But I think he's mistaken. It was a story about his brother's ex-girlfriend, a story about his nephew. He died of mad cow disease. A story of bad meat & bad beer. A story of DUI or nephews without fathers. But it's so tragic, your uncle with an estranged daughter. The shunned wedding. Or the long drive to funerals. // All those empties on the floor tell a story. // Another High Life, compadre? Another Michelob Ultra, compadre? Dos Equis or Bohemia? // Wasn't that girl arrested for dealing last year? // There's a lot of fire in the backyard. A pit of fire. // Aren't there enough men spinning yarns, thumping drunk guitars. // That sizzle of beef sounds tasty. // Some cops want to shut us down. // They say go home. Go home to your loneliness. // Oh sorry. That was me. I did that. // I sweat tears. I burned myself. I don't want to brag about your PlayStation 2. I don't want to brag about another dare. // Isn't it true, all those years ago? // Too stoned to see anybody else. // Crouched beneath the park in swim trunks, weren't you, too, a small boy once? // Kissing a girl twice your age. When she stepped out of the pool. There was no tongue. // You'd believe that? // How many birthdays did you forget? // How many of them blurred together? // Every year they say you're tall. // Maybe this party is a reunion, your birthday, a Fourth of July party. Another quince. // Maybe the family just likes to say things. // Isn't that funny, your friend says, there's some child inside you asking, Why blow out the birthday candles at all? //

SELF-PORTRAIT WHILE HOLDING MY MOTHER'S HAND

Distant thumbprints
on yellowed documents.
        Blue ink of her father's hand.

From the great beyond, my mother
hears ghosts. *This is what is left of us.*
        Her parents willed blood into a document.

Their last testament: *You can have this plot of land.*
But dirt doesn't always obey.

In the time of narco wars,
her sister warns her

of the impossible task,
        to claim the last piece.
           She must make it worthwhile.

What does my mother think
        of the place she leaves?
        I catch her voice

trembling for the small sum
        she can pass to her children,
        who whine & can't afford

ties to apartments.
        In six months, I must leave this place.
        In the time of children

at serrated borders—
        my mother still has pride in
        what she can offer.

Her parents knew
anything was better than nothing.

This is her last chance.
My faith in her, bound by birth.

At sixty, my mother wants to hold
       her right hand up, swear to God &
       say, *I am a citizen.*

       What's left for me
       must be held as prayer.

Her motherland.
       Her childhood.

       I must listen to her.

THE LAUNDROMAT SAINT

The way Mother folded
    my clothes.
    I still don't know what I'm doing.

My hands could never be as good.
    Eight years old, I'm with Mom at our laundromat,
    a handful of quarters to keep us busy,

                       a gumball machine,
                       a knob that turns,

    a Snickers bar,
    a can of store-brand root beer,
    a little wrestler in his tiny plastic dome.

I pat my pockets
    for a prayer card from my mother.
    It lives there.

Here, a man in the rear works evenings
    while I thumb prayers &
    coins & sink into a rhythm.

His hands, chisel & chisel curls off
    slabs of wood.
    Mother of God,

the man carves saints into this shape:
    Guadalupe, Lupe, Guadalupe
    I hum with care while he works

endlessly. He blows the sawdust away.
    I've been waiting for my mother's hands
    to fold me all along.

SELF-PORTRAIT AS MY MOTHER'S BLOOD

I take myself out some Saturday mornings. I order chorizo,
carne al pastor, tortillas & eggs (so I can make breakfast as she did).

These, I pack inside an icebox
with cold drinks for a long roadtrip, a cookout in Austin.

& when I can no longer drive,
I become like my father on a family trip.

Sleepy boy, I park under the glow of America,
no trees can cover me:

only the lot's radiance washes over.
When I arrive, I call her for advice.

When she answers, I'm back home: her voice.
Eres mi Hijo, she tells me.

As if we were always tied together.
As if I never moved across the country &

it feels right—like shopping with her
at Walmart on Saturday for groceries,

so when I say I was young,
I learned to miss the word *mother*.

Because I began saying *mom, mama, mother*
to the stars & they answered

even when I was far away
shopping at the carniceria.

PORTRAIT OF WHAT HE DIDN'T WANT

Don't you wish you could live a life you didn't want?

Once, in a tall office building—the city below glowed
fluorescent. Hallways illuminated a tunnel toward

quiet. Toward a dusty man's perched office.
Overlooking the streets, my father wears his jumpsuit.

Green or gray [memory is funny], his vacuum is dirty & cleaning.
He didn't picture children in his life. Before construction,

his hands did whatever life dealt him.
On a table, my father plays Texas Hold'em.

He's not a betting man. Neither am I.
Only hold what you see in front of you, he'd say.

Lately, I think my father is afraid of the future.
He won't divorce my mother. He'll fold unto himself.

He'll insist on carving his space inside a corner of our house.
All his life, he's been cleaning corner offices.

He piles new clothes, new teeth, new hair—trying
to look as handsome as someone else.

He calls me, wanting to become whoever I am.
I'm *Pedro Paramo*. He tells me. [A character in Juan Rulfo's novel.]

Nobody ever wants to be Pedro Paramo. He's awful, I say.
        & he doesn't mind. He likes thinking of himself as a ghost town.

He has his own apartment now. He wants to clean his sins.
He's grooming himself in the mirror.

Complaining about the mess in our house. He built himself
a new bedroom. A separate apartment he locks away from us.

He's such a neat man. He sees mess where my mother has already mopped
the floors. The sheen of tile on his forehead. He didn't want to pick up
the pieces. He didn't want love to become backbreaking work. He didn't
want that choice. One day, he found himself with a hammer. He didn't
want to clean houses. He filled himself with things. All the things he
never had.

At sixteen, my mother woke me & the night felt like a secret. Hushed & opaque. I was the translator. Between bail bond & county jail. I don't want to know your world's hush. Don't want to wander in your criminal or drunk state. What keeps you away, so quiet, drinking without us? Driving home, you were stopped that night by sirens. Mother always said you were with someone else. Someone else was calling our house & you weren't here. Silent ghosts. Haunting. I always wondered, what if you didn't come home one day & it didn't feel wrong. The slick shape of a home. Where have you been? [Mom says you were with someone in X. Was it Tulsa? Weatherford. Wichita Falls.] Were you with a secret family? [I never knew for sure.] When you disappear, I'll end up working. Working all night to keep a roof over our heads. You asked me once—what would happen if you were gone. As if death would leave us prisoners to your absence. Inside a locked room, you hide the dim, blue light of your texts. But you love us. Indeed, you love us. We are still waiting for the divorce. Waiting for the afterlife. You ask me: *Am I a good father?* What if I could unfather you. What if I could see what kind of father I'll raise. When you're my old man, what are we going to do when you're hurting & I'm washing your old body because you can't.

I'll scrub you, Father. I'll become less like you.

WHEN FATHER SINGS

after Michael Salgado

Let the tequila flow,
my father sings,

like holy water over my grave.
When I leave you, pour the bottle out like a farewell.

Some mornings his ghost sings:
When I leave you. Celebrate me, invite everyone to clink spirits.

Once, I woke from a dream where
he died & I sobbed.

Let the box be cheap, he sings.

Once, on the balcony of a hotel,
he admits in song:

When I pass, don't bury me
in anything, I don't deserve.

What my father carries is a tomb.

The shadow of grief won't be worth it.
This burden you should unshoulder.

& I do, Father.
I'll hear your *gritos* still,

not from a grave but from my own throat.
I hear your newborn burden & sing it.

PORTRAIT OF A BOY RETURNING TO DIRT

We drive south to Laredo from Dallas.
    We pull into the lot because
        the rest stop resembles
            a restless pit of dirt.

My father wants us
        to *know*
            his home.

Processed & waived.
        The border is
            so much waiting.

So much to confirm:
      origins, passports,
            our other homes.

        Finally, the desert,
    the lonely tolls.
Checkpoints with portraits of Mexico,

      mothers & their children.
        They wait for someone

to buy their pan dulce,
      their mangos
            spiced with lime juice & chili.

We eat where we come from.
    We drive through the ranged
        mountains & see

fields of wheat. My father's dirt.
      My foot remembers
            stepping down

            from his pickup
      into his village.
I'm a small child now

      greeting *my* grandmother,
            my grandfather,
                  my father's playground.

      Where he said
      I had nothing but this.

STEPPING THROUGH A DOOR

Before I was born, my father
putting himself inside a Chevy Impala, his body

hunched in the trunk, hiding,
            listening to the freeway until the coyote

turns up the radio & lets my father passenger up
            front & says *You look Chicano enough.*

            The keys becoming his.

Chipped, worn, jangly like a rattle,
            his hands buckling us into child seats.

We're watching him turn dials.
Michael Salgado. The news.

            In our sleep,
we're wishing they reported on immigrant fathers

like—*immigrant father teaches his boys to grow arms
long enough to turn any frame into an invitation.*

Half asleep from reading all night,
            my father stepping into the frame,

checks to see if we're sleeping
            like American boys. The distinct musk of work.

I miss it. In those Forest Lane apartments—
            we're waiting for his gifts through a magic door.

            His hands covered in plaster,
saying *I will unlock anything you ask for.*

THE HOME SLAUGHTER

The first time I see an altar,
I carry a six-pack & float to an island.

I came here a student of history,
ready to unroot. What was Mexico like? I wondered.

How did my father & mother once
watch the smoldering remains of a goat offering,

how did their fathers & mothers drip & pool
the ritual? Memory rotted & threaded through me.

I arrived here to ask about origin.
Who were your fathers & your mothers?   I dream:

Donde estas, mijo? Donde aprendiste?
Mother asks how did I learn? *Ritual,* I say.

Grief, I say. I take my family's money
& I'm guilty

inside a mezcal-lit Mexican bar, eighteen years old.
A woman holds her pinky around mine,

we're walking down the aisle—marrying.
What does it mean to make dreams?

Your home—where it smells
like cajeta—or the sweetness

of visiting my father's home,
where a pig snout nuzzles me.

Me, a small boy saying
      the slaughter of pork

      soup, bone & broth——
tastes like tears.

      & I listen again to my father.
His words: *my village*, he says. *My father*, he says.

      Imagine my father staring at the tarmac
waiting with me for a flight to Dallas—

      where he knows he left the past
to make ends meet. He will break

      open the ground.
Hammer & cement my feet.

      He will carry my soft boyhead into our country.
Call me on the phone & ask if I'm alright.

Hold my voice & ask
how I slaughter my hands into dreams.

SELF-PORTRAIT WITH THUNDER & EXHAUSTION, OR
SELF-PORTRAIT AS MY FATHER CROSSING

Sudden thunder & a spell of rain.
Full night widening its throat.
Soft music inside a black car.
Rivered roads & thick rain.
The warm LED of Motel 6.
You want headlamps & roads.
Stars to hang like bright molars
scattered. Orion's chest slit by
the white knife of a half moon.
If your eyes are heavy,
picture an open ribcage,
a fistful of blood. Become
one with the sternum of the road.
Nod off.
What brought you here?
Something restless.
Something dark.
You will follow
its shoulder.   You will go empty
with high beams. The middle of
nowhere.   Nobody but silhouettes.
Trees rustle in the wind, whispering:
Pray for lightning.   The hazards blink.
On & off. Off & on.
Engine hums & faith will keep
you throttled.   Keep you from skidding.

Let the sky be yours.
Go home. Kiss the mouth of dawn.

YOUR PORTRAIT IN SMOKE

Off the coast of Texas, say your father
never waded the waters. Say he left you &
he stayed with G's mother. You'd play
two-player games on the weekends.

That's your brother leaning close like a father.
He teaches you guitar & you want to lasso
every word with a guitar string.
You want voice.

You want wood smoke.
A wood that doesn't judge
your ax coming down
sharp on the dead.

Say there's a lovesick lyric
your brother sings about country
& home. They say there's a next life

where your soul burns white-
hot like the moon. Tomorrow's a snake fang evening.
You dream you knock its teeth out.

You say you mourn all life.
You say thank God your boot spared you.

Thank god, the phoenix rises & eats the flesh
of the serpent you once harbored

tight around your heart. Your shadow won't win.

Even when your sins are there, bleeding all over the place.
Even when they say they'll always love you.

You won't know any better than your shadow.
You won't know if someone is gonna shoot you.

You'll pose for family
with enough will to live with that blood.

You won't realize
your body is a fable

until the earth is burning
where your feet once stood still

the peak of life ahead of you
& the fog of another asking your heels to dig in harder.

What did he want?   I don't know.
What she wanted: Perhaps, she knew.
When born, I did   what the body understood.
Brothers will do   what brothers do. Put on want.
Are families what   tenderness lacks? Understanding
doesn't ever come   easy. Easy is what we don't do.
Pushing what isn't   hard aside, measuring what's left—
that's what I don't recognize yet. The softness
of bodies holding   until the family becomes tender.
Ready the blood.   Ready the picture, hold still.
My father never   knew what he wanted
until his firstborn took a breath, wailing.
My mother knew   nothing of God until she prayed
& asked God what   does God want?

FOOTAGE OF ME TOMORROW

I

I consult   the deck.   my friend
stars   palms.   I'm   half
empty   I see my father
                    I see   a   Flamed

                        forest. Watch   that   Quiet
laughter   echo
my
            stop being a bird.

                              desire

                  listen   I didn't learn
                                        anyone else's life.

        the moon   card
                                  Two people   fall.
                                    how many
                              means whatever I want

                                  I mean   I
        Muddy your
                                              Father.

II

I   shuffle the
stars &   pour   half
                                                                    my father
                                                      in a jar

         There's   Quiet
          Abundance. I have a long heart
my   love
   ain't easy   It's messy

            you'd have to be a fool.
                 To
                      listen   I   learn
forgiveness   inside my father's   life.

When   I play a game. I'm drawing   a tower
                                                      falling or about to fall.
            with sudden   fires
I'm   Snake eyes. It means

       anyone can   die   tomorrow
yesterday   inside a cup you turn
             dark   say I'm   my father.

III

I consult the tarot. I ask my friend to shuffle the deck. I consult my friend who reads
stars & palms. I contain possibilities. I'm the glass poured half full or half
empty. I need perspective, my friend tells me. What do you see? I see my father
carrying ten swords. I see Venus entering Pisces. Forgiveness in a jar. Flamed

memory. There's a Joker in the forest. Watch out for that wild card. Quiet
laughter. Abundance. I have a long heart line. I've been echoing
my father. From birth, I wondered how much—we love freedom.
It ain't easy to stop being a bird. I'm one boy learning to fly. It's messy.

To want the sky you'd have to be a fool. To desire anything,
I have to dare myself. To squander time. I won't wait on myself.
What I mean is, I haven't listened for a long time. I didn't learn
forgiveness. I'm inside my father's sitcom. Streaming anyone else's life.

When the moon is full, I play a game. I'm drawing a card. There's a tower card.
I'm drinking liquor. I see lightning strike. Two people falling or about to fall.
When faced with sudden heights, I want to know how many fires await me.
I'm rolling the dice again. Snake eyes. It means whatever I want it to mean.

It means anyone can cast the same die twice. It means tomorrow is what I drank
yesterday. Muddy your coffee grounds inside a cup you turn upside down.
Chunks fall like the dark slipping away—they say I'm not my father.

NOT PICTURED:

[This isn't his father's first rodeo.] The second son was born one winter. Picture that son entering the frame, maybe ten years old—it's 1998 [& he never saw the first rodeo]. Hotter than a rattle in the yard, snaking toward the father's ankle. [Have you ever seen thunder that close?] What sweat does—makes imaginations go black & blue. [Mamá, esa noche—so many candles & prayers]. Lovers so many years ago— [During the father's first marriage]. Picture the State Fair of Texas October—a happy family—drinking so much water from the concession stand. [*Have you ever seen the rain?* faintly pattering the pavement.] Crowds of legs, walking from stand to stand. The boy holds hands with his two parents. [Find one sibling—missing.]

The father will dare the son, the distant speaker of this poem, to sip his first Lone Star, his first Corona, his first [taste of blood—his first teeth bleeding or] feasting on a turkey leg the size of his head. [Your brother is missing.] He's riding the Gravitron. [Insert voice-over from the present that misremembers the family's first Kodak memory: *spinning the way a child travels. Around and around and back home again. A place where we know . . .*] That son was loved. [Insert soundtrack—*what would you do if I sang out of tune.*]

Enter the family dinner—or [outside the frame: *cannibal-fratricide*— chew on the photograph of Brother—missing] picture them inside the family Suburban—Father cutting his fajitas on a sizzling skillet. A boy's mother is knifing open his enchiladas—red saucing his shirt. [Blame everything on the weather or the father's raising.] That winter they posed for the family photo. [Your brother sleeps above the second son, who looks up—watching the brimstone.] Only the burnt wick remains.

II

BURNING

You have to think of me what you think of me. I had
To live my life, even its late, florid style. Before
You judge this, think of her. Then think of fire . . .

—Larry Levis, "My Story in a Late Style of Fire"

It's true, we don't see family much. // There aren't any pools anymore. // We stopped playing music // together. We don't bother inviting your uncle, he's sad. // Don't trust anyone anymore. // I don't think your brother is coming. // We don't sound like we're alive, do we? // There's tenderness in the pantry, I think. // We're too old to make tamales. // Nobody wants to learn how. // Is that a good enough reason to say no? // None of us will have children. // Do you wonder if they're afraid of becoming bad fathers? // Why don't you ask your mother about that? // I stopped drinking beer a long time ago. // We're getting a divorce, Mijo. // How come you're always bringing someone different around? // Why can't you settle down, Mijo? // I'll do anything I can for my kids. // _____. // Tell your brother happy birthday. // Tell your mother happy Mother's Day. // Que Dios te salve, Maria. // No te dejas caer de la tentación. // Understand me when I say this, Mijo, I want you to be happy. // You weren't raised in a barn. // What would you do if I wasn't around? // What would you do if your brother was here, right now? // Why don't you stay here tonight? // Your mother made too many. When are you going to learn to make tamales at home? // Why do you only call when you need something? // Don't get so nervous. // I'm sorry I screamed at you. I love you. // I'm sorry _____. // I'm sorry _____. //

In a stale marriage, my father hides
cradling a vow to father you. Do you wonder

if knew we'd become brothers?

We could still forgive these promises, Father.

We could dig a grave—& yearn
        for something taller, grander than marriage.

SELF-PORTRAIT LOOKING BACKWARD

I stopped looking at your photo
I can't remember what your face looks like
Never have I cherished something so dear
Your face like a sun against morning
Your face like a full moon, looking down under streetlight.
Didn't I tell you, I loved too much.
Under the awning of a diner on the Upper West Side,
it's raining. I never told you how lonely I got
when I entered the fluorescent booth &
I asked for no toast. Just eggs,
sunny-side up with bacon.
I pepper & salt the meal,
& I add a dash of hot sauce.
My fork splitting the yolk,
I'm eating alone
across the street from a place
where I'm lucky to have a bed.
By myself. You warned me,
I shouldn't stay.
Except, I didn't listen
when you said it's over.
I became so sad, I became a tear.
I became so thin, I drank only beer & you worried about my bones.
Then I couldn't breathe.
I thought I was dying in the cab,
clutching my chest—then I saw my father
departing the gate, flying away with me to Texas.
Falling asleep,
departing the gate, flying away with me to Texas.
Clutching my chest—I saw my father
dying in a cab. Then he couldn't breathe.
I could drink only beer. I became so thin, you worried about my bones.
I became a tear, I became so sad,

you said it was over.
Except, I didn't listen.
You shouldn't stay
by yourself. You warned me.
I'm lucky to have a bed
across the street from a place
where I'm eating alone,
my fork splits the yolk.
I add a dash of hot sauce.
I pepper & salt the meal
sunny side up with bacon.
I asked for no toast. Just eggs.
When I entered the fluorescent booth,
it was raining. I never told you how lonely I got
under the awning of a diner on the Upper West Side.
Didn't I tell you, I love too much.
Your face like a full moon, looking down under streetlight.
Your face like a sun against morning.
Never have I cherished something so dear.
I can't remember what your face looks like.
I stopped looking at your photo.

MY MOTHER'S BLESSING

Always a sign of the cross
on my forehead—

There are afternoons
she brings a recycled bottle

of Ozarka spring water—
she fills it with holy water,

her index & thumb
splash grace there

because she won't let
her husband's sins

poison me, she wants
God to protect & bless

me from the wickedness
of vice. She calls him

pig, demon, wailing
in the streets,

stinking of perfume,
not hers & she wants

to wash it away; that's why
she throws holy water at him & me

because we won't be good men,
we won't be as good as the father

who speaks for God
with his sermon &

I always want to line up
for the body & blood,

but it's been years since my last confession
& I don't know where to begin, Mother.

PORTRAIT OF MY PARENTS' DESIRE

Let me begin by looking in the mirror. You recognize
your mother's chin & nose, your father's neck &
his vanity. Once upon a time, they found each other.

> They say it was a holiday party. Employees were invited
> to a ballroom. It was 1987. Big hair. Your father's swagger
> danced your mother into an affair. They tell you little

> > of your circumstances. They say no one wants
> > to picture the conception of their birth. You just *are*
> > one day. You don't wonder why your mother prays

> harder every day now. She once loved a man,
> now you're living. Now she doesn't love him anymore.
> You wonder if she wonders if it was worth it.

You remember her dreams. Her fairy tales whispered
to you at bedtime. La princesa de la casa wants to cut stars
from dark linen. Cut out the other woman. Never pictured.

> Only heard. Peeking through a window. You ask yourself,
> Brother, if you wanted him to fight for her longer. Have you
> > ever seen a man love so much?
> His bare hands clenched for this family.

> > In the mirror, your face like a father's asks:
> > *Am I my father's love?* Look into your eyes.
> > The way light hits, reflects, and betrays.

Your family jokes you were born a bastard.
Bastard. You learned the word from them.
Your father, your brother——they're pulling your leg.

It's a ribbing. Feel that elbowing deep.
That scar on your head. Blame your brother.
He's jealous, your mother would say.

Pray your father loves you just as much.
Comb your hair just like him. Wear his work shirt.
Smell like him.

Looking in the mirror, you practice saying *I love you.*
over and over and over and over again.

PORTRAIT OF MY MOTHER AS THE LOVE EMBRACE
OF THE UNIVERSE, THE EARTH (MEXICO),
MYSELF, DIEGO, AND SEÑOR XOLOTL

after Frida Khalo

What I see:

My mother cradles my father,
& the moon & earth & the planets.
She looks down while the heavy arms of night
& day coddle him. In this portrait, we belong to the universe.

In this poem, we see what we want. Mothers with motherhood
& far away from hunger. We desire a space

for this strange tenderness.
This portrait is nourished by the embrace of what little we have.

See the cacti & hardy plants—they hardly thirst & are largely rootless.
They are thorny, spikey things. I welcome their touch.

Look, we can make the father a baby.
Innocent & holding his paltry fire flowers.

Her solemn eyes see straight through,

as if saying *don't become dead-eyed like your father.*
& I want to say what Lorca says
that only Mexico can grasp the hand of death.

Pictured here: Xolotl, usherer of the underworld,
I found out he's the brother to art & composition.

& like my brother, I want to hold him.
Like you're holding our father, our mother.

Listen to his sleep, his thunder breath.
That's what I'm staring at on the computer screen.

That's what I want to see.
So I change my mind & begin to see myself

as the rich, wet maw of Mud,
as the dead tail of a dog, wagging.

AFTER *EL HOMBRE* BY RUFINO TAMAYO

What if I wore nothing but bark.
    A tree,

        the people's shadow,
the loom over loam.

        Who says the earth was solid
        like bedrock or

soft like mud.
    Who wouldn't

        learn to plant their feet
            deep until there is

no tug when pulled.
            Why not root here, let my arms

            branch & reach
            for constellations,

      a language fit for yearning:
What will my fathers say,

            when you, my son, cut me to a stump?
    What dog will stay with me

          when touching the sky
    feels distant like memory?

Chocolate flowers' bloom,
      tell me what does the sky say now

when days grow darker,
when we wonder
          what kingdom will remain?

BIG TEX IS ON FIRE!

On October 19, 2013, Big Tex, the iconic fifty-two-foot
cowboy, caught fire at the State Fair of Texas

Size 70 boots, 75-plus-gallon hat since 1952,
he says—*Howdy, folks!*
Welcome, boys & girls! Welcome to the State Fair
of Texas!
Imagine you're a small boy, by his feet.
Then an electrical wire shorts one day.
He bursts bright like a saint.
They once hailed Big Tex the saint of corn dogs.
Your brother from another mother
eats corn dogs with you &
you both run away from flames.
Maybe it was divine intervention.
Maybe some beautiful kind of disaster.
Iconography you can burn onto your eyeballs.
No, votive candles.
No, God says, *It's time.*
The police say *They've got a tall cowboy with his clothes charred off.*
Everyone says *Howdy, howdy, folks. It's hot.*

Oh, Brother—you're sad.
You forgot to say it back.
You forgot to visit Big Tex all those years.
He's like your Uncle Lalo.
The one you still think of—his Fourth of July parties.
Y'all watch him paint grief on murals,
the back of warehouse buildings.
All his children half-siblings
because he became a widower twice—
had children you played with because
families are hard. He's the only other artist
who understands picking up the pieces

becomes a strange art.
Oh, Brother—you're sad.

                                      Have you ever heard your Uncle cry,
                                      calling your home, waking your father?

Grandmama passed
& she won't ever know the disaster our family has become.
                                      Lay it on me, Big Tex.
                                      Take a brush, paint him burning.

Make his face *your face.*
Turn him into an effigy.

                                      Tell him you hate this city.
                                      Tell him it doesn't matter what he wore.
Imagine brothers playing with lighters.

    Oh, Brother—we're sad figures—

                                      learning to greet flint with amazement.

LOST FOOTAGE OF US PLAYING

I hate pictures of myself. Not because
I don't like the way I look

but because I stopped paying attention.
Before, my brother & I

played with the family camcorder.
The sun always caught us, bright.

You couldn't see our faces flashing.   We had to wait
for everything to adjust.

Then we'd act out our favorite
martial arts scenes.

He's the Karate Kid. I'm Zorro.
He's the Blue Ranger & I'd become "Stone Cold" Steve Austin.

We'd be wrestling over who loves Dad more
            [That part is left out.]

What wasn't captured, our feelings.
It's not like when the disposable camera

caught us: birthday cake on our faces,
we're shirtless boys, thumping our chests,

screaming. We are two years apart—
we drift away: graduations—big moves,

life zips by, like my thumb scrolling through the feed
searching for your photos, Brother.

I must ask: If there's no photo to document
our family? Are we living?

       Am I letting go?

I can't remember the last time
I saw myself smiling with you,

but there's a laughter
in the corner of memory—somewhere

the distant bright yards & Dad mowing the grass
remind me of days I was once level with you.

STUDYING ABROAD IN MEXICO, LOOKING UP AT *MAN OF FIRE* BY JOSÉ CLEMENTE OROZCO

Through a ceiling, the sun's flames
shine through the *Man of Fire*. I saw him once.
En la Plaza de Tapatía, I wandered the streets
of Guadalajara in July, an inferno. My feet burned
& my head burned & I was wiping sweat when I
saw him. He was a human torch. His gray hands
reached for mine like he's not sorry.
Is this my father's love?

His hands reddening me, whooping his fears out,
burning flesh with anger—hot tears asking *why me.*
Why smolder when the forests are going to ash.
This isn't about the world aflame. My own house
has never been set ablaze. Though, I've seen smoke.
My mother chars peppers with enough heat it licks
my tears, makes my lungs scream. Orozco's flames
were bigger than that. *Chiloso* or *invincible*, my father
never called me those things. He could never stand
the kitchen. Because I was jacketless in winter,
trying to prove I didn't need anyone, my father
called me IceMan. The way I stood in Guadalajara,
its cantinas, lighting cigars, foolishly—so I could
tell him—*don't extinguish this tall licking flame.*
I want to die slowly—like murals peeling from the ceiling.

FOOTAGE OF MY FATHER TELLING A STORY ABOUT DIRT

Tell me the story again

        how you shaped clay into a toy.

All you had was dirt.

        Such an old thing to have.

I didn't believe you

        until I visited your childhood fields.

You have the same bones

        as your stern father,

your stoic mother.

        No wonder you ran away.

I don't wonder anymore

        why you go to work

for the grocer, restless boy.

        You killed boredom.

You pictured the sky

        as more than a field of wheat.

I didn't know you, Father.

        Were you too busy working—looking

beyond the pasture?

        In the beginning, there was a story.

You placed us like dolls

        inside a fenced backyard.

My brother & I once played
           those figures in the shadows.

As dinosaur, as transformer,
           as figures of action for the rivalry

clawing deep like memory
           or digging out the dark.

Black crescent moons
           under our nails,

I want something
           to uncover, to tell my children

what I lacked like my father.
           Like a magician,

I will pull the thread of my father's thirst,
           & teach my children to thirst

for the blood of an open field
           leading back to their grandfather's grave.

WHEN FATHER & I SPEAK

// You always were a philosopher. //

I came here for better opportunities.

I ran away from home & lived inside the grocer's mansion.

// Or you were bored. You always told me el rancho was never for you. //

Because I didn't know better, I crossed a border more than once.

Then you were born & I wore my hands out for a job I never wanted.

// You got caught. //

I wanted a better life for you. I promised myself, I'd be a good father.

// I asked what were your dreams & you said you never asked for anything. //

// We watched the movie A Better Life, *starring Demián Bichir & we cried
at the end. We cried together. //*

FATHER'S ADVICE

He said, *Don't be a burden,*
& he climbed the scaffold.
He turned the heavy wheel
of work. His *day-laborer* title
became one worthy of a desk:
Boss. We never understood
what it took until later;
we, siblings, found how
he ruined his hands
into blisters for a living.
How he built houses,
plastered walls, & reached
for the bluest ceilings.
He never complained
because his blood
must be worthwhile,
must not be left
behind a fence.
When he comes home,
his gray sweat pours a foundation.
We become cemented to his dirt,
this roof over our heads.
My father says:

Others might want the ground we stand on.
Never look like you thirst—

his words were a slab
for an ugly home. Finally ours.
His advice is less tool-like,
more father-like, I disobey him
when I want more. I am not a father yet.

Instead, I call my roof a burden.

FOOTAGE FROM THE FIELD

Half lit by cars, we flick cigarettes in the parking lot.
You point to spokes & spin them, open the hood, & I see

my father there. You turn the engine on: *Turbocharge*,
you say. O'Reilly's. Back to a slick-floored garage,

we're under the car passing tools as father & son.
He'd say it takes a little grease & elbow.

We keep wiping the hood down.

He tells me to hand him the tray. Oil pools between us.

We keep standing there, ash & beer swished in our mouths,
waiting to spit under the moon's head.

                                   Halogen glow of the driveway.

I remember what I once was—like a moth
drawn to my father's vices, his breath—

Check your fluids, he'd say.
Check the tire pressure, he'd tap.

THUD. Tension. At any moment,
a blowout. A swerve off the ready-made path.

I still wrestle with doing right. Following directions.
Knowing the machine. Torque & fuel—

which bolts do I tighten? Every dent, a former doubt.
I pay attention so I don't go sobbing

when the tires go loose

                          & question *when do I become myself?*

SOBBING IN A U-HAUL

Like my father, I left behind dreams written inside notebooks,
my childhood boxed inside a garage. I sold the car he bought me:

a Ford Mustang, coal gray like the Wisconsin skies
over Lake Michigan, which froze

while I stared from its bluffs in winter.
I lived here once. When I told Dad

I'm leaving,

he looked at me.
He let my hands go

with the keys to the truck,
an embrace that felt sorry

to watch me move on—unloading
what I once believed was important:

my bookshelf, desk & coats.
He always says *don't carry what you cannot carry later.*

& I keep leaving things behind, learning. I sat sobbing
in a U-Haul on the phone with him in a parking lot,

loving & losing. Each time I lose, I lighten my load.
I fill my body with his voice.

DIPTYCH: DREAMS ON FIRE

I

I wake up sobbing. At twelve years old, I find myself in Anaheim.
We're on vacation. There's a train running through my head.
My father stalls at railroad tracks in his blue pickup truck.
Ask me what he said earlier, when we stood thinking of our Disney
family adventure. It stayed with me—*what if I wasn't here*, he said.
Looking over a balcony, I ask, Was I always afraid to lose my father?

> You should know my father was an angry man once.
> I saw him make a grown man cry—*I'm sorry I screamed at you.*

He calls me back to say. *I'm scared you'll fuck up like me.*
I'm just a dumb Mexican. Aren't you supposed to be smarter than me?

I'm sorry there's a welt.

II

I woke crying for him because we were
driving on the High Five Interchange.   Until we weren't.
Twelve stories up, we lost control. I know we're not dead.

I'll reach for my phone to call him. He'll answer.

He won't know why I call—that I was afraid.
He wonders when I'll call him because

I spend so much energy only to have nothing.
Just relax, he tells me. *Just relax*, he says.

Don't worry so much. He worries so much, I know.
We're outside. He's working construction.

He invited me here. He's wearing a hard hat. He's drinking water.
He offers me some too.

MY FATHER NEVER SPEAKS ABOUT HIS FATHER

except to say, he ran away from him
    at thirteen
    to live in a grocer's mansion.

He left behind his father all those years ago.
I watch my father sob for the first time
    when I raise a fist against him.
    That night, his fury asked,

Was I a good father?

I am thirteen & dreaming of a dead father—
    train wrecked in a pickup truck. Wake up, teary-eyed boy.
    Later, over a balcony. He asks,

What if I were gone?

There are nights I lay awake asking myself too:

    Am I a good man? What if I were gone?

What is written about fathers is in our DNA.
    It is a small childhood fury.

Where I take my fists to pummel my brother & question
what is fair?   [When I expect my father's attention—]

I can make my father cry.
How did he get so fragile & distant,

as if the sky could bear his dreams
& ours—or pull the moon down with a rope.

My father, my father, I'm shaking with gratitude.
When can we abandon hurt—become the blazing eyes of burning.

BLOOD & BREATH

Somewhere, years ago, I ate dirt.
Somehow I forgot this dark.
I forgot beginnings. Who recalls
the earth's birth? Years go on.
We become ruins, dust—oblivion.
The first brothers' wisdom was to kill.
Soil the ground with blood. First breath
taken. Is this blood a curse? I ate it.
When it rains, I pray it will wash off.
But the sun continues rising &
stories return & return us to dirt.
We squint at the familiar unfamiliar.
How does the animal kingdom know
what is right & wrong? What is north
& south? Do worms know the light?
What would it be like to feed like one?
Know nothing but the drain of rain.
How was I once a boy, fighting like
birds do, over who could kill the snake?
My brother did it with a small stone.
After a storm, I stepped on
the sidewalk. The blood of worms
went unnoticed until I bent down
& watched nature ravage its body.
I'll die like that one day or soon. Pass
like years, like nothing was ever there.
What am I capable of, dear brother?
All I know is we are here loving &
forgetting until one of us dies
by chance. I must risk it all then,
so I can make some small impression.
Like the first brothers who were or were
not there. Some sorry storied breath,
whispering dust to cosmic winds.

FOOTAGE OF ME YESTERDAY

I

You saw me pacing the room. You saw me calling my mother. You saw
me calling my father.

You saw me eating with my brother. We ask if we remember the footage
we shot. We hit pause.

Zoom in on that booger in our nose. Close-up sound of laughter. That
time I slept beneath him.

Bunkmates. Sometimes I wished it wasn't just weekends. Sometimes he
was my brother.

Except—we weren't invited to the wedding. He might not read this. I
might say I didn't

mean it. Except, you can see me pacing my room. You can see me leave
him on *message read*.

I know you're watching me make choices. You're watching me keep our
ties cut. Yet,

where do I point the camera? Where does the plot end? I can't press
record.

II

pacing the room   calling my mother
calling my
             brother   we remember the
      pause.
                                                  That
time I
             wished it was   just weekends.

we were   invited to the wedding. He might not

mean it.   You can see me

             make choices.
      Yet,
where do I   plot   ? I can't
      cord.

III

                    pacing   my mother
              calling my father
        eating   my brother. We hit
Zoom
          I slept beneath

          my brother.
Except—   the wedding. He might   read this. I
      might
mean it. Except, you can   leave
      him
I   make choices

                    Where   the plot   can't press
      record.

IV

my mother

my father.
my brother.   remember

laughter.

the wedding   I

leave

V

                                                  my mother

                      my father.
                  my brother

                              Close

PORTRAIT OF US BURNING

If the morning scaffolds, then night prayers come.
If years ago, Mother & Father ate only rice & beans,
then we slept in one bunk bed & Saturdays were
for chilaquiles & Sundays for church—weekly buffets
& big screens, the dollar theater. We grew quiet.
If we filled our evenings with silence, they yelled.
In the car, in the bedroom, in the dining room—
we held on. We hold still. It costs something
to be something. Like Father said, *It costs money*
to breathe. I catch Father coughing cigarettes.
His eyes worry. Like flames. His throat was on fire.
Screaming. Just yesterday, he said I should *work*
harder. As if he didn't break his hands enough
when I asked to borrow from him. Again, I am broke-
n, a fragment of him, of Mother—her voice
will worry too. As if I never caught her, years ago,
lighting a cigarette or caught ashamed raising
her hand, saying *I'm sorry, I'm sorry, I'm sorry.*
As if she could be a better mother. As if
she never flew across the country for me,
to the sixth-floor walk-up of my depression.
She sang *arrorró mi niño, arrorró mi sol, arrorró*
pedazo de mi corazón & I was no longer twenty-five.
I was a boy, burnt out & afraid my heart would give
in & give me nothing. Nothing for all those years
Father whooped me with a stick, a belt, his working
hand. Oh, what a storm. Him medicating his anger.
What flickers between us now. Me, sparking up
a calm. Days ago he called to apologize for yelling.
He remembers rage when he chased me before I left
& as I climbed the fence to say I would leave this roof.
I wonder what we learned. What did we sing in our hot
breath? What did we say then? What do we say now,
holding our frustrated, flaring hearts?

EVERYTHING IS ON FIRE

Even if the fire was set
before us,

like a spell to vanquish
the father, could we learn

to love its ashes & ruins?
Couldn't that mean

we're free to vulture
over the scorched earth?

Thank you, Mother.
Thank you, Father.

All the bridges are flames.

Isn't it time they
tell us a story?

Once upon a time,
we watched an inferno dance

& we saged the house
& we lay in the yard

& we saw the meteors
hot in the sky

& that's how we learned
God wrote love long ago

during the big bang.
He let the stardust explode

& folded the dust inside
a sheet of paper.

Set it free like a plane,
zipping through stars.

Its wings flickering
with the scent of burning.

WHEN MY MOTHER'S PORTRAIT SINGS

When she prays in the living room.

When her son leaves the house.

When she puts her head down, chanting rosary after rosary.

When she gifts him sweets, her pozole, anything for her firstborn.

When she signs the Father, the Son & the Holy Ghost—she wants
    nothing.

When she wants nothing but steamed salmon—vegetable medleys in
    February.

When food reminds her of Acapulco with her sisters; she says she always
    loved the water.

When was the last time we took her to the beach?

When this wasn't quite the sleepy nursery rhyme she sang to her son.

When her son doesn't understand there are no fairy tales.

When there is no one but God waiting.

When we both listen to el Padre say only God can judge.

When at night the family dog barks at the door & the mother shushes
    her like a daughter.

PORTRAIT OF FAMILY AS A BAG OF WORMS

As a boy, she kneaded the ghosts from my belly.
I found faith in the body. Como los gusanos.

Como time crawling & ticking away like wrinkles

or pimples I want to squeeze.   Pero Mamá,

te dije que eres mi sangre, mi santo siempre.
Madre, mi noche.   Mother, my night.

Saturdays at the Chinese buffet,
my family opens their fortune. Driving back to suburbia,
my father fights with my mother.

There's another woman.   There's a question:
Why haven't we left him yet?

Pero Mamá, me dijiste en aquellos días:
Sana sana, colita de rana. Meaning,
heal, heal, the tail of a frog.

                    Next Sunday
we'll go to Good Shepherd & ask for forgiveness.

Let me heed the father's words when my mother
presses her thumb against her index—like a cross.
She prays I don't burn like my father's desire
in the back seat, sitting with me.   Brother, I'm sorry

I'm speaking to you like a stranger.
You slept above me & called my mother Lala.

When we were young, we slicked back our hair
some mornings. Dad would say,   *let's play the Texas lotto,*

like my mother lighting money incense.
& the smoke sings, if we don't heal today,   we'll heal tomorrow.

(Si no sanas hoy, sanarás mañana.)

As if healing was as simple as my mother rubbing Vicks on my chest.
As if an ointment could soothe this open wound, Brother.

When the family portrait omits someone—
When the picture is marked incomplete—

When there's a gaping hole, *agape* enters my mouth
& my learning remembers the word's Greek origin:

unconditional love from the Father—God,
family—endless affection.

As if there was a circle
around the portrait—as if my mother never cut him

out of the frame. As if I never drew worms
in blue ink—coming out his lips.   Two horns

away from being little devils, sometimes   I drew them on myself.

PORTRAIT OF FAMILY II

My father wants to have it all. The house with the yard,
two Dodge pickup trucks & a Christmas tree every year,
lights flashing *Feliz Navidad,*

próspero año y felicidad & us singing *I wanna wish you a Merry Christmas.*

For us to be whole & gushing, I wonder if there must be a blade
coming from the bottom of our hearts—must we take it?

CAJETA

We always wanted a family. Didn't Father beg
for us to act like one? He yelled at us to make
plans. Don't take your sweet time. Don't get thick
with me. Didn't he mean for his efforts to yield
better blood than before? Richer than before.
We are rich with family. He says *we're fine. We're fine.*
Yet his body tells me it's tired. Tired of the molasses
of burden. Not sweet anymore, it burns. My mother's
burden was once slow too. In Celaya, city of candied milk,
she loved cajeta. How it simmered good & overnight.
A cosmetology graduate. I once misunderstood her
as someone who studied the stars & it ended up
true anyway. She dressed & cut our hair for family
portraits. The star of Texas & cloud played backdrop.
Her baby's first hair was sweetened inside a plastic bag, a drawer.
Something to burn the past in our hands when we hold it,
simmering like birthday candles. Remember, mama y papa:
Pastel de tres leches. Cake of three milks.
We put frosting on everyone's nose. Remember, Brother?
Why don't we gather to make plans? Why take so long
to meet once a year around a table—why not feast & drink
about the dreams we saw as boys, climbing our city's roof—
when we didn't know how long fireworks lasted because
we lay there under July for what seemed like hours &
we joined the family & ate fajitas & drank soda & ate cake
& we even felt like a family, rich & without burden.

STILL-LIFE WITH SALT ON FRUIT

In those days, mi Mama me dijo
There wasn't enough salt.
But we were grateful. Agradecemos.
En aquellos días, my Mom was enough.
We sat at the picnic tables in Duck Creek Park.
Mis tías, mis tíos, we all loved simply.
Skirt steak on the grill, tortillas on the comal.
We tended fire until the embers had enough heat,
until we could dust salt & chew fajitas &
my siblings & cousins could run rolling
down the hills of the park. Texas sweat
on the rim. Big Red in Solo cups.
Easter Sunday after Mass, we'd come back here.
My brother's birthday in August, we'd come wild
again. Enough to forget Six Flags, fighting,
the Chuck E. Cheese pizza & games. Grass stains
on jeans, our mom said we ruined them. Her wet
hands would scrub & scrub, detergent & clean &
clean. The same hands that could take a knife
& present her sliced cubes: the bright juicy red
of *sandia*. Cut & displayed for our summer treat.
A veces, we came to the backyard. In our tire
swing, we sat eating fruit. Sticky sweet fingers.
Blazing drops of sweat on our shirt. She'd bring
the watermelon drizzled with salt & chili powder,
the night draping its curtain. What laughter.
What treasure. Mom would say *eat, eat*, there's more
now & more later & we siblings would come full
& now I am staring out the yard telling my mother,
look, I have more than enough—I can cook
what you taught me back in those days.

WATCHING THE END OF THE FILM *PARIS, TEXAS*

(dir. Wim Wenders)

My father never left me in a burning house. Lately, I've been thinking about the unconditional. How many fuckups are tolerable before someone gives up or stops loving. My father still loves me. He still loves my brother. My father did leave my brother behind. His home wasn't burning. No, his heart was sweating for my mother, once. Hand to God, hand to glass, I don't know if I know this love. One that stays with me. In the film, Travis, the protagonist, must make a choice. The estranged mother must make a choice. It must be hard. In this proem we can say everyone wants love. I've never visited Paris, Texas, but when I saw first saw the film, it struck me—how far away they all were from each other—in time, space & feeling. Opening shot: a man lost in vast country—Texas. Empty of people & streets. He seemed so small. Thin almost. He wore grief like an old cheap bag. Sun-blistered. This man holds weariness like I imagine my father did when he climbed out the trunk of an Impala. On his side of the family, the men are quiet in their work. Quiet with sweat. Somehow they afford to say so little. I must be honest,

I'm afraid I'll become my father—running away from everyone. In a video recording my father sends me one Christmas, he looks into the camera: he says he's sorry he wasn't a better man. He's sorry. He's convinced himself he wasn't good enough. See, I once pictured my father walking up to my brother's mother years ago. I don't know when he told her about me. I don't know if it was easy or not. I don't know if I can see my father like Travis, pressing his hand to the glass, saying he often dreams he is on fire. He admits he was afraid of responsibility. In the film, Travis says he froze. His wife, his children were on fire. In my version, my father ran away from Mexico. I picture Travis wearing my father's eyes—afraid his wife will leave him. [I don't know why I'm telling you this, Brother. I don't know what it's like for you.] See for yourself—what silence makes a father do. Watching the film, I begin to wonder, what speeches did your mother practice for our father, Brother? When she was mad, she didn't just take it, did she? Just like Travis, your father left when the heat got hot. What if things were different, or what if we didn't try to paint over what was or could've been? I don't think our father would run away now.

I don't think my brother or my father have seen *Paris, Texas*—if they did, I'd watch if they follow the camera panning across the landscape. I'd like to find myself reclining with a beloved I won't leave. We're climbing onto a bed & I'd like to think we have no regrets. Oh, desire, desire, desire—an engine for a better life—if I could speak a letter into a telephone & promise to receive nothing in return

FORGIVE ME, BROTHER

There was a meadow.
I told myself there was a mountain.
Your mother shot me.
I didn't die but it hurt.
Daddy went to jail
& you slept above me
in your bunk. Gnarled
vines when we talked.
We cried.
You told me a story
about a witch.

[I forget context.]

She rode her car into the moon.
We couldn't trust her.

[Or could we be wrong?]

What if she's not to blame,
what if beneath a mountain
there's a man.
Our father, an eruption.

Remember our father's
pistol? In her hands, a disaster.
In her hands,
flowers, petals
falling. Forgive me,
Brother, we are nothing
but forgiveness.
We are days
since then, leafing

toward sky,
our fists can open finally,
palm our father's
boyhood, a thing we carry
dormant like his kiss.

DISTANT FATHER

Don't make me repeat myself
I'll tell you if it's pointless
that bruised slumber of youth
like a dream I keep returning
to the stoplight where my wound
was held, the hospital where my head bled.
I begin stretching myself into a truth so tall,
I outgrow its sleeves.
My father's jacket, I once wore
what felt like years of his sweat,
all those toiled days labored for
his boys. If I'm repeating myself,
it's because my father asked the soft-spoken boy
that I was years ago if I could repeat myself.
If I drink enough wine with him these days,
I'd realize we're not so drunk anymore. Sober,
I'll watch him ask for another. His smile
will call back his younger self. Neon boy

at the jukebox. Silver truck ready to take
anyone home. If I'm repeating myself,
it's because I don't want to ask strangers
for a kiss—when I picture myself my at father's age
I'm asking if I'm my father's son. If I'm asking you
what I really want to ask—what kind of father will I
unearth? Because if I bury mine, what use is this story?
If I'm repeating myself, it's because I'm not a boy,
I'm not simply a half-sibling, I'm a brother. I'm a son.
I'm crafting a sharper profile of where I've been & I'm an arm
lifting a dollhouse on my shoulder for a child—elsewhere.
If I'm repeating myself, it's because I'm carving a figure;
I'm a father using his teacher voice. I'm in the passenger seat
speaking with a good friend. We're driving to the mountains.

He's in love with his wife. I keep asking him to tell me
what is that like? I keep asking because I want to look far away
thinking of what I'd do with such a thing—how does it look
when I'm imagining a child who doesn't think I'm not so awful.

THE OWNERSHIP OF THE NIGHT

after Larry Levis

1

I'm twenty-five in the kitchen of my parents' house,
staring at cabinets like they can recognize I've become
distant from the teenager I once was—reaching for the late-night
bag of popcorn. Now, I nest under an infomercial asking me
to *act now, before it's too late* & I wonder how I've returned
to the mosquitoes' buzz in humid Texas, where I don't
want another routine to save me. Those beasts savor
my blood anyway. I wonder how the 1-800 number
can still insist life is worthwhile.

2

Years ago, there was a woman. We went to the beach.
We looked over the bluffs & stepped into a void.
When we listened to the lake & saw the vast dark except
for two ships anchored, their lights pulling farther away.
Confusion. The sheet of waves & stars seemed to beat on
until suddenly a girl I didn't know came in search of a lost baggie
of weed between crags; below the pier, we stood on. We walked away
because we didn't like the way it felt anymore. Instead, we slept at the shore.
The next morning we saw a bonfire pit abandoned in the sand. Nothing could
stop us from making love there in the bushes, unsatisfied with the way we lived.

3

This evening I picture those moments as bridges
where I walk hand in hand with lovers & friends that I let go of.
They are distant like ghosts. What transpires is a photograph
that never feels quite present or near. I wonder how to capture
the shot of me then, six years ago. How do I hold on to these snapshots,
these versions of me? How do I project the one I want to become?

Any one of them could be a stranger laughing hard. This one too,
I can't help that it looks like a silhouette of a younger me,
one who looks like my father—slipping into fog. What if
I'm like him? Lighting the last of a cigarette—becoming night.

ACKNOWLEDGMENTS

Thank you to the editors of the following journals, where poems originally appeared or are forthcoming, sometimes in earlier versions and under different titles:

Bennington Review: "Forgive Me, Brother"

Blackbird: "After *El Hombre* by Rufino Tamayo," "Self-Portrait with Thunder & Exhaustion, or Self-Portrait as My Father Crossing"

The Cortland Review: "Cajeta"

Cosmonauts Avenue: "Footage of My Father Telling a Story about Dirt"

Crazyhorse: "Footage of Us Playing," "Hibiscus"

Front Porch Journal: "Diego Rivera, *The Flower Carrier*, 1935"

Hobart: "Portrait of Rivalry"

Kenyon Review Online: "Portrait of a Boy Returning to Dirt," "Self-Portrait While Holding My Mother's Hand"

Lunch Ticket: "Where Your Mother Was"

Missouri Review's Poem of the Week: "The Laundromat Saint"

New England Review: "Blood & Breath"

New South: "Dear Father"

North American Review: "Where Your Father Was"

Pilgrimage: "The Ownership of the Night"

Prelude: "Portrait of a Reunion"

Salamander: "Portrait of Us Burning"

Salt Hill: "Self-Portrait as My Mother's Blood"

Southeast Review: "Studying Abroad in Mexico, Looking Up at *Man of Fire* by José Clemente Orozco"

Southern Indiana Review: "Everything Is on Fire"

Southwest Review: "The Home Slaughter"

32 Poems: "Father's Advice," "When Father Sings"

TriQuarterly: "Footage from the Field"

upstreet: "Self-Portrait as My Father, the Roofer"

Waxwing: "My Mother's Blessing," "Still-Life with Salt on Fruit"

Deepest gratitude to Marisa Siegel and the editorial team at Northwestern University Press and Curbstone Books for believing in *Portrait of Us Burning*. I'm also grateful to editors Jenny Xu, Lisa Ampleman, and Marianne Chan for offering feedback and guidance to bring this book where it is now.

I'm endlessly grateful to the University of North Texas, Sarah Lawrence College, the Bread Loaf Writers' Conference, and the Sewanee Writers' Conference for their resources, instruction, and community. I'm especially thankful for the mentorship of my teachers and for their support and belief in my work: Brenda Cárdenas, Tina Chang, Cynthia Cruz, B. H. Fairchild, Rachel Eliza Griffiths, francine j. harris, Edward Hirsch, Eileen Myles, Marilyn Nelson, Urayoán Noel, D. Nurkse, Matthew Olzmann, Victoria Redel, Patrick Rosal, Brenda Shaughnessy, C. Dale Young, and many others. Special thanks to my dissertation committee, Jehanne Dubrow and Corey Marks. I'm very grateful to Bruce Bond, my first college poetry workshop professor and dissertation chair, without whom I couldn't have made the decision to pursue poetry. To the late Thomas Lux, who was my thesis advisor and an example of what a poet could do with words, and who told me he'd kick my ass if I stopped writing poetry and, I believe, would come beyond the grave to do just that.

I'm incredibly lucky and grateful to the friends I've made along the way on this journey and extend my deepest thanks to those who read drafts, shared support, and offered insight, especially Taneum Bambrick, Gabrielle Bates, Dorothy Chan, Dolapo Demuren, Mag Gabbert,

Shannon Hardwick, Jenny Molberg, Dustin K. Pearson, B Rivka, Esteban Rodriguez, Michael Shewmaker, Mike Soto, Alina Stefanescu, Paul Tran, Emily Jungmin Yoon, and thank you to Jim Redmond for shared friendship and support. Sincerest gratitude goes to courtney marie and Spiderweb Salon for their space and community over the years. Thank you to the support of my workshop members and especially to my fellow Bread Loaf waiter and staff crew whose conversations and shared support indirectly shaped this book.

Special thanks go to CantoMundo, the Vermont Studio Center, and the Dobie-Paisano Fellowship Program's awarding me the Jesse H. Jones Fellowship at the University of Texas at Austin and the Texas Institute of Letters for the space, time, and community it offered to me. I'm thankful to have met Brian Van Reet and Michael Adams on the ranch.

Many thanks to my family for their love and support over the years. Thank you to you, dear reader, for picking up this book.